The Cry of the Magpies

The Portable Library of Korean Literature

The Portable Library of Korean Literature introduces readers
around the world to the depth and breadth of a vibrant literary
tradition that heretofore has been little known outside of
Korea. These small books, each devoted to a single writer,
will be appreciated for their originality, for their universality,
and for their broad range of styles and themes. The goal of
The Portable Library of Korean Literature is to bring Korean
creative writing into the mainstream of world literature.

—Korea Literature Translation Institute

The Portable Library of Korean Literature

Short Fiction · **3**

The Cry of the Magpies

Kim Dong-ni

Translated by
Sol Soonbong

Jimoondang Publishing Company

Seoul · Edison

The Cry of the Magpies · Deungsin-bul
Original title: Kkachisori, Deungsin-bul
© 1961 Kim Dong-ni
© English translation 2002 Sol Soonbong
All rights reserved.

The Portable Library of Korean Literature is edited
by the Korea Literature Translation Institute.

Acknowledgement is made to *Korea Journal*
for permission to reprint the texts.

Jimoondang Publishing Company
95 Waryong-dong, Jongno-gu, Seoul, Korea
Phone 02 743 0227, 02 743 3192-3
Fax 02 742 4657, 02 743 3097
E-mail jimoon@shinbiro.com / jimoondang@yahoo.com
www.jimoon.co.kr
ISBN 89-88095-58-8

Printed in Korea

Book design—CHUNG DESIGN

CONTENTS

The Cry of the Magpies

One day while I was looking over the new books section at my usual bookstore, I caught sight of a thin book entitled (*Give Me Back My Life*). There was a subtitle: *A Confession by a Murderer.*

"*Give Me Back My Life?*" I asked myself and picked up the book. I opened it and started reading the preface. I soon came to a sentence which for some reason gave me a mild pang in the heart. It read: "I too had dreamed of becoming a great writer, but war left me branded as a murderer." I had of course heard similar such things said elsewhere, and often, too. So I cannot explain why I was especially moved by that particular sentence on that particular day. It could be that the key was in the "I had dreamed of becoming a great writer" part of the statement. Maybe it aroused in me some sort of a fraternal feeling.

I bought the book and finished it that very night. It was a moving and thought-provoking story. The style was quite good, too, maybe because the author "had dreamed of becoming a great writer."

I will reproduce here the story I read that night. In doing so, I intend to stick to the author's own words and expressions as much as possible, because they are really quite remarkable. The book opens with his description of the village where most of the events take place.

In the center of the village was a well. Two aged pine trees stood, one on each side of the well, raising their gigantic arms and staring at each other. The trunks with rugged bark were very thick; one would have to stretch one's arms several times their length to go around the entire circumference of each tree. They were hollow inside on the lower parts, and a dark mysterious silence filled each hollow. Compared with the thick, rugged trunks, the limbs and the foliage were on the meager side. One of the outstretched limbs had been broken in the middle. And one could see that some new branches had come out on the broken main branches. Yet, instead of stretching upward toward the sky, these secondary branches were drooping downward, their scanty leaves hanging limply.

The good main branches, however, soared high like

flags flying over the shoulders of two giants. And there were many side branches laden with healthy leaves.... It was on these branches that the magpies had built their nests.

There were three nests, one on the tree closer to the road and two on the other one standing on the opposite side. Nobody knew the exact number of magpies inhabiting these trees, nor did anyone know since when the magpies had nested in them. Maybe the villagers merely assumed that the nests had been there from time immemorial like the trees themselves.

Nor was there anybody that knew the origin of the belief among the villagers that if the magpies cry in the morning there will be guests or good news that day and if the birds cry in the evening there will be a sudden death. Regardless of who started the superstition, the morning magpie cries did seem actually to bring guests or good news, while the evening ones seemed often to forebode death. So the villagers were inclined to believe in this superstition.

Meanwhile, the magpies cried in the morning, in the evening, and at any other hour that pleased them.

"Bong-su!" she would call to me, and then invariably add: "Kill me." She would repeat this routine every time the magpies' crying caused yet another of her horrible, choking cough spells from which she nearly fainted. Once her coughing started it would go on and on as if it would never end. The coughs came in a sound patterns of: 4-4-2-1-6, 3-4-2-6, as well as other combinations accompanied by all kinds of rhythmic variations. Such exclamations as *O! Ah! O-o-o!* or *A-a-a!* gave further complexity to the coughing. Anyhow, it was only at the end of these spells of coughing and fainting that she recovered enough breath to go through her "Bong-su! Kill me!" refrain.

My mother's coughing started about a year before I was drafted. So one could say that the illness was almost three years old by the time I returned home from the army. Only, the coughing had by them become far more painful and habitual.

According to my sister, Ok-nan, my mother began to expect me home the very day after I had left. That morning the magpies had cried in the old pine trees, and my mother had abruptly said to Ok-nan: "It must be your brother coming home!"

"O, Mom," said Ok-nan, "how can he be coming home when it was only yesterday that he left?"

"But don't you hear the magpies crying in the trees?" My mother would not give up hope.

From that day on, every time there were magpies crying in the morning, my mother would fret, expecting me home any moment. When this had lasted about half a year, the fretting began to turn into most excruciating coughing spells.

Although I said "about half a year," this should not be taken too literally. Ok-nan said that her coughing fits had occurred even before the half year had elapsed. When months passed by without a word from me and the magpies continued to cry in the mornings, my mother's eyes began to glare in a strange way. Then the strange glaring of her eyes seemed to shift over to a long spell of coughs. At first her condition was not so very bad, but beginning about one year after I left home, she got to coughing almost without fail whenever the magpies cried in the morning. Then later on, she got to coughing every time the magpies made the least sound in the trees, regardless of the hour.

But I think this is all quite understandable. I mean the fact that my mother's coughing fits worsened in that way after her hopes of seeing her son had been so consistently frustrated. It is in fact easy to imagine how the cries of the magpies, especially the matinal cries, had become an unbearable reminder of her frustration and disappointment, and how this could have led her already existing condition of coughing to turn into a permanent condition of a most painful type.

I think, too, that there was good enough reason in her calling out her son's name and imploring him to kill her after each excruciating coughing spell. I remember my mother was in the habit of mouthing such words as "O, God!" or "Help me!" after her occasional coughing fits even before I left home for the battlefield. And now she was replacing those words with "Bong-su!" and "Kill me!" In my view, there was not much inconsistency in this development. Rather, these seemingly contradictory expressions were no more mutually exclusive than the two sides of one coin. The way I looked at it, "Help me" could very naturally become "Kill me," as suffering deepened into bottomless despair.

So during the first days after I came home from the war, these words, or rather entreaties coming from my mother, filled me with unbearable sorrow and rage. The intensity of the emotion was so extreme that my limbs shook from the tension it created.

"Oh, that she should suffer like that!" I said to myself, "that she should have missed me so much!"

I used to be so sorry for her that tears filled up in my eyes when I saw her suffer like that. And yet, there was no way in which I could help my mother in her suffering. For one thing, I had no money to let her get any kind of medical treatment. My sense of helplessness made me feel more guilty about her suffering. And I suppose nobody would find it difficult to see why I felt that way. And so I continued to suffer and agonize along with my mother.

Then something happened. Some strange change took place in me. For some reason too crazy for me, or anyone, to understand, I began to feel an impulse to kill her. As I said before, I knew well that when she said, "Bong-su! Kill me!" it was not to be taken literally. It was an emphatic expression of her wish to be "saved." I knew all this very well. Then why was it that I felt like killing her?

And this was not an impulse that came to me just once and then left. Once it started coming, it came back all the time. When the magpies cried and my mother's coughing started, my eyes began to glow strangely, as Ok-nan described them. She said that on those occasions my eyes gleamed the same way my mother's eyes did when she had first started to cough to the cawing of the magpies. Somehow when my mother's coughing reached the point where she nearly fainted from panting and choking, I found myself swept away by an impulse to lay my hands on my mother's emaciated neck and strangle her.

I think this mad impulse hit me the hardest the first few days after it's initial occurrence....

I remember the impulse was so strong that on the

third day, while desperately struggling to repress it, I took up and threw down a water bowl that was lying beside me, shattering it to pieces on the floor. On the fourth day. I went as far as to lunge toward my mother, who was on the verge of fainting as usual. Just then, however, Ok-nan ran into the room and threw herself on me, stopping me in my crazed pursuit.

On the fifth day, I did not even have a chance to…because, who was standing near by, ran in just as the magpies started cawing. I restrained myself for a while but, when my mother's coughing went over into the fainting stage, I could do so no longer. Ferociously I pushed Ok-nan, who stood between me and mother, onto my mother and ran out of the room kicking the door open with my foot.

I think those five days were the worst period. After that, whenever my mother started coughing, I managed to run out of the room without waiting for her "Bong-su! Kill-me!" although by that time Ok-nan was standing between my mother and me, anyway.

This precaution on my part, however, could not be completely dependable. One could easily imagine situations which would prevent my leaving the room in time. In order to make my point clear, I will have to explain the layout of my house, though I feel a little bit reluctant because it is such a small house, too small for decent human living. There was a three *pyeong* room, which is fair-sized by countryside standards and yet small nonetheless. Then, there was a barn on one side of the room and a kitchen on the other. This was all. So the three of us had only one room to live in. Suppose I get drunk or something and have to stay in the room the tomorrow, I asked myself, would I be able to act swiftly enough to leave the room the instant the magpies started cawing?

One more strange thing was that as soon as my mother's coughing stopped and I could regain some calm, I began to have doubts about what had just taken place. Did it really happen or was it only my imagination? Could it be that I had hallucinated?

Meanwhile the cawing and coughing went on and I usually succeeded in running out of the room before the thing I so dreaded could have any chance of happening.

The turmoil in me, however, did not easily subside merely with running away. Hearing her panting and gasping from outside the room was, if anything, even worse than being with her in the room. My body kept on trembling from this unbearable tension and extreme stress. The one consolation in suffering outside rather than inside was that I now did not have to worry about strangling her. Instead I unleashed my pent up fury on our dog, Blackie, whom I kicked and beat in a total frenzy.

Yesterday I broke a wine cup in the village tavern. I was rather tipsy at the moment and was feeling pretty disgusted with the person I was drinking with. And yet these were not the reasons why I broke the cup. I mean I had no perceivable motive for breaking it, and the occasion certainly did not call for such a disruptive act. What really happened was that the blood leapt to my head when I heard the cry of the magpies which had started just then. My limbs began to tremble and I dropped the wine cup I was holding with wine still in it. No, this is not how it was. The fact is that I didn't really drop it but must have hurled it down onto the ground. Otherwise, the ceramic cup wouldn't have split right down the middle as it did.

I have been suggesting that I was victim to some irrational compulsion which was beyond my control, but in doing this I do not intend to shift the responsibility away from myself. To clarify this point further, let me explain how it was that I got so inextricably, and so insanely, involved in my mother's coughing. Before I go into any further explanation, however, I must declare that I never hated my mother. Not ever. Rather, my love for my mother had become, after my return from the army, much deeper. On the other hand, however, I had gradually come to the realization that her "Bong-su! Kill me!"

was not merely a senseless iteration born out of her suffering. Several times, I heard her say: "I ought to be dead so Ok-nan could marry and you could bring your bride home," and I suspected that she meant what she said, at least partially.

Ok-nan also helped me guess the real significance of her habitual iterations. Ok-nan told me that, while I was away in the army, Mr. Jang proposed to Ok-nan but had to be refused because she could not marry yet, at least until I came home. This was the reason she gave to Mr. Jang when she refused him, but the real reason, Ok-nan said, was that she could not bring herself to marry and leave her ailing mother alone, who needed all the care her daughter could render her.

Talking about Mother's sickness, Ok-nan said that that was what really lay at the bottom of Jeong-sun's heart when she broke off the her engagement with me. Everybody heard that Sang-ho was constantly reminding Jeong-sun of the fact that all she could hope to get after all the waiting she did for me was nothing more than the burden of caring for a sick person. He went so far as telling her that I got killed on the front and showed her a forged official notice of death in action. In this way, he succeeded in tricking her into marrying him. If all this told by Ok-nan were true, however, Jeong-sun's marrying Sang-ho had not been through persuasion, but by downright deception. What I am trying to say is that she did not go back on her word because of my mother, but because of the forged death notice. That is, my mother was after all not much responsible for my broken engagement. I did not in any case believe that Jeong-sun ran away from me because of my mother. All the same, I am not going to deny that my insane response to her coughing had something, however little, to do with Jeong-sun(and Sang-ho).

Anyway, let me tell you everything, everything that may have any bearing on my reactions to my mother's pitiable ailment and her verbal appeals directed to me. When I got an honorable discharge from the Army and came home,—yes, this is where I should begin my story. I will make the moment when I re-entered our village the starting point of my story. The first thing that came into my sight were the two ancient pine trees standing in their old places by the village well. Ah, how I had missed the sight of those trees! And they were a sure sign that I was back on my homeground. I can't quite explain why I felt so moved by the sight of those ungainly-looking trees that were maimed and blackened with age. At the very least, however, they were an integral part of my memory of those dearest to my heart: my mother, Ok-nan, and Jeong-sun. Also it could not be denied that the trees were a symbolic representation of all that our village stood for. (*Oh, you dear, ugly, old trees of my childhood, tell me, tell me, how is everybody, mother, Ok-nan and Jeong-sun?*) Asking these silent questions in a lyrical vein, I walked into the village.

I enumerated "mother, Ok-nan, and Jeong-sun," but, honestly, the order should have been: Jeong-sun, mother and Ok-nan. Then, it would have been truer to my feelings. In fact, it was solely for Jeong-sun's sake that I returned alive to my old village. To say this, I know, is to commit the sin of unfiliality toward my dead father and ailing mother and also to betray my love and duty toward my only sister. But I cannot help it. What plucked me out of the jaws of a certain death on the battlefield was the thought of Jeong-sun. There are things I need to tell you about this field of death and my escape from it, but we'll come back to it later on.

Anyway, I thus made my appearance before my mother and sister like a long-awaited savior(at least in their eyes). As I approached the village well where Ok-nan was rinsing barley corns, it was Ok-nan that saw me first. For a few seconds, however, she merely stared at me without moving. Her eyes had gone vacant as if she could not believe what she was seeing. Next moment, however, she sprang up with a cry: "*Oppa*(a term used to designate 'brother' but also often used by girls a women when addressing boys or men older than themselves).″ She ran up to me and buried her head in my chest sobbing unrestrainedly as if forgetting all her innate bashfulness in public… As for me, I merely looked down at her almost like a stranger, like a man who could not feel.

I noticed that she had grown into a beautiful young woman during the year and a half of my absence. How could a young woman so pure and beautiful be so happy to see a beggar like me, a beggar in tattered fatigues! Then I remembered that she was my sister. Yes, my sister! She is my sister! And that's why she is crying like this. With this thought, a prayer stirred in me of its own accord: "Please, be happy, my sister!"

We walked home together. The bareness of the yard gave me a pang in the heart. Not that I had expected to see sacks of grain stacked up there or anything like that, but I was nonetheless pained by the poverty of our house as I looked at the empty yard.

"Mother! *Oppa* came back!" Thus crying, Ok-nan pushed the door open, overjoyed to be the announcer of my arrival to our mother.

My mother abruptly raised her body from the waist up. Her wrinkled face had no flesh to it at all. Her two sunken eyes, however, were aglare, and with those glaring eyes she kept on looking up at me. Still she did not say anything. Maybe she was afraid that speaking might cause her to cough. She sat up on the bedroll with her mouth half open and one hand on her chest.

"Mother," I said.

I put down my olive-colored army bag in one corner of the room and, kneeling before my mother, kowtowed. I did not ask her how she had been or how she was feeling now. Why bother? Couldn't I see the answer right before me? Didn't her face tell of nothing but suffering, poverty, loneliness and despair?

"How was it in the army? Weren't you very hungry?" She finally risked a few words in a panting, phlegmy voice.

I did not answer her. As if in anger, I just sat looking at the opposite wall without a word. What have I brought her? Have I even brought back the body she gave me intact? Have I brought her money to treat her illness? Have I brought even a pair of those colored rubber shoes which would have made Ok-nan happy? They didn't know yet that I had not even come back for them. They didn't know that it was only for Jeong-sun and our love that I cheated the army, betrayed my country and came home, stealing away my life.

"You had better lie down, Mother, lest the coughing start."

Ok-nan helped her lie down on the bedroll, embracing

her by the shoulders.

"You must be tired from the trip," she said, turning her head to look at me. "You ought to rest, too. I will get dinner ready soon." Even as she said these words to me, I could see that she was deliberately not looking at the army bag I had put down in one corner of the small room. I knew that she was curious and expectant of its contents, and I decided to reveal them all at once. I did not want to let the poor girl nourish any hope on what the bag might have....

"These are the blanket and the uniform I used in the army," I said, unpacking the bag. I then produced my underwear. With these out, the bag was nearly flat. Nothing much was left. There were two pieces of chocolate, two packs of chewing gum, a pack of candy and a few items of canned goods, all of which I had stored away from the ration I got in the army. There was also a pair of liver-colored wool gloves, made in U.S.A., which an army friend of mine had given me when I left the hospital. I pulled all this out and laid it on the floor.

But there was still one more object in the bag. It was wrapped with wrapping paper. I did not disclose this even to Ok-nan. It was a red sweater which I bought with the money I had saved from the paltry sum I had received from the army for the trip home. This was the only thing I bought personally. Of course, I did not tell this to Ok-nan. Besides this, moreover, I picked up one of the chocolates and a pack of chewing gum from the floor and put them back in the bag, saying, "This is all I have with me. Mother might like some of the canned goods. You eat, too. From the rest, take whatever you or Mother can use."

Ok-nan said nothing; she had been without words the entire time I was unpacking. I read resentment in her eyes that seemed to be avoiding mine.

"I have nothing else for you, but you understand, don't you?"

"Oh, I don't mind, but—" Ok-nan did not complete whatever she was going to say. Instead, she left the room.

Just as I expected, she is offended, I thought. She must be angry thinking I have something fantastically good for Jeong-sun. That's why she said "I don't mind, but..." She probably was going to say I should have been kinder to Mother. She meant to wreak her own resentment on me in that way.

I shoved the scattered things toward my mother and, using the folded army blanket as a pillow, lay down on the floor. I thought it was natural my sister should feel offended, but there seemed nothing I could do about it. So I decided not to dwell on it any further.

After having finished the meal, which was both lunch and dinner for me, I pushed the wrapped gift along with the chocolate and the chewing gum into my coat pocket as best I could and sauntered out of my house.

"Wait a moment, *Oppa*," said Ok-nan, who had been washing dishes in the kitchen. I stopped.

"Sister Jeong-sun," Ok-nan hesitated to go on. At once I had a presentiment of something bad in her tone. Maybe the fact that my sister hadn't mentioned Jeong-sun at all in the long while since I had arrived home that afternoon made me sense it the more quickly. I waited.

"She got married," said Ok-nan at last.

"She did what?"

Alarmed by the sudden ferocity that came into my face, she hung back, but after a few seconds, as if she had made up her mind to have it done with, she said, "To Suk's brother."

"Suk's brother? You mean Sang-ho?" I said.

Not averting her steady big eyes from me, Ok-nan nodded.

"But how could she..." I mumbled weakly and stopped.

"It seems he got her to marry him by deception. He told her you were killed." Ok-nan tried to console me.

"What? He told her I was k-killed?"

Even as I asked this question in a trembling voice,

however, something in me seemed to be agreeing, that I had indeed been killed on the battlefield. A strange sense of self-defeat and self-derision replaced the shock and anger of a short before. Maybe what he said about my being killed was right, after all. I felt like laughing.

"He told her you were killed in a combat and showed her a notice or something which supposedly came from the army." Ok-nan's voice was shaking with anger.

Suddenly my head swam. If Sang-ho had been there at the moment, I am sure I would have killed him right there and then.

The next thing I knew, I was running out of the gate without a thought as to where I was going. When I had left our alleyway behind and reached the road where the pine trees were standing, however, I stopped short. Then, almost at once, I felt a hand on my arm. It was Ok-nan. She had been running after me, it seemed. . . .

"Let's go home, *Oppa*," she said breathlessly pulling at my arm slightly.

As if spellbound. I allowed myself to be dragged along by her in the direction of our house. What else could I have done anyway? Was there anything for which I should have shaken myself free from my sister's restraining hand? No. There was no such thing. It was as if "I" had ceased to exist. If there was an "I", what would "I" have thought or what should "I" have done?

Anyway, "I" did not exist at the moment and that is why I surrendered myself to Ok-nan's frail hand for the time being.

I entered the room and lay down as Ok-nan advised me to. At the other end of the room my mother was lying in her bed. So we lay there together in one room, each turning towards the wall. I kept my eyes closed but was far from sleeping.

The sun went down, and dusk fell. There was a breeze beginning to stir in the cool of the evening. My sister finished the dishes and made two trips to the well. Although my eyes remained closed, I was well aware of what was going on.

The magpies started crying. My mother sat up, coughing. Although those two things happened simultaneously, or rather, successively as if on some previous agreement, I did not know then that there was some connection between the magpies' crying and my mother's coughing.

I waited patiently, my face still toward the wall, until the long, obstinate coughing spell was over. I raised myself up from the floor only when my mother finished saying her "Oh, God," "Bong-su, kill me!" I did not do anything to make it easier for her. I could have stroked her back or done something placatory like that. But I didn't. Nor did I say anything to console her. I left the room without a word.

It was quite dark outside. I could see a star giving out bluish light between the branches of the leather tree in our yard. I went out of the gate, but was soon caught by Ok-nan, who had been talking in whispers with a girl about her age by the hedge.

"Where are you going, *Oppa*?" she asked.

I did not answer. I merely tossed my head back once.

Whether or not my sister divined my intentions, I could not tell. She said, "This is Yeong-suk," and pointed with her chin to the girl standing before her.

Who can she be? I wondered for a second and was about to move on. At the same moment, the girl my sister called Yeong-suk turned to me and lowered her head in greeting. She looked a couple of years younger than Ok-nan. She had a slim body and an oblong face.

Who is that girl? Wondering, I started again, still saying nothing. Then I heard the girl's voice:

"My brother's not back from town yet."

At once I realized the girl was the sister of Sang-ho, my enemy. She was still a little girl with a pretty, egg-shaped face when I left for the army. She used to run around after me as if she were my little sister. "She must be a sophomore or junior in high school by now," I thought vaguely, and resumed walking.

"Don't you have anything to say to Yeong-suk,

Oppa?"

Yes, I now recognized her oblong delicate face with a fair skin. She used to call both Jeong-sun and Ok-nan "Sister" and was with them much. But I was the one she liked most. She was, it seemed, of a different breed from the rest of her family. She must have run over to my house as soon as she heard the news of my homecoming But what words did I have for her?

I walked away, not saying anything to her, but then I remembered I did have something to say to her:

"When your brother comes home, will you tell him I want to see him?"

"He'll come to see you himself, I am sure," said Yeong-suk in a calm, clear voice.

I started walking toward Owl's Corner. Although I did not doubt the truth of what Ok-nan told me about Jeong-sun, I wanted to hear the story directly from her own folks.

There were her mother and older brother, her father having died early. The brother was almost old enough to be her father. I always called him "Yun's father." In our part of the country, there was no such a thing as an engagement. People went straight to marriage from courting, so to speak. Since everybody knew about Jeong-sun and me, we were as good as "engaged." So I really should have called him "Brother" but for some reason I didn't. Now I was going to his house to have a word with him.

Yun's father was glad to see me but he didn't say anything about Jeong-sun. He merely kept on asking things about the war. Although I was not in the mood for a chat, I answered his questions dutifully. After I had emptied the second bowl of rice wine that he poured for me, however, I asked him directly:

"What happened to Jeong-sun?"

"Well, yes, so you see…" he mumbled on these senseless words instead of giving an answer to my question. Then, he said, "Let me pour you some more wine," and poured the liquor into my bowl.

"You know," he went on, "I don't take to drinking much. One or two bowls are more than enough for me. Tonight I have had far more than I should, just for the pleasure of sitting with you. So, drink, man, don't let me get drunk all by myself."

What does all this talk about drinking have to do with Jeong-sun? I felt exasperated and barely kept myself from putting the same question to him again. Instead, I drank the wine he poured into my bowl in one gulp.

"You are the brain in our village, aren't you?" he said. "You can go up to the capital this minute and can study at the best college there without paying a cent—what do you call it, a scholarship, is it? You would even be able to save up some money from this scholarship and send it back to your folks, am I right? Good brain, good looks, bound to end up as county chief at the very least. What's a president, what's a cabinet minister, what's a country girl to you? Nothing. What man would refuse to give his daughter to a young man like you, eh? Would a girl like our Jeong-sun matter to you then? There will be dozens of city maidens dying to marry you. Am I right?"

Finally I lost my patience. I could not sit and listen to his rigmarole any more…

"What happened to Jeong-sun?" I asked the question I had asked before.

"Jeong-sun? She got married to Sang-ho. He is one for whom Jeong-sun is perhaps good enough, eh? But not you, no sir! You could have had any girl you chose in the village, couldn't you? Such a bright, good-looking, well-mannered young man like you—You were quite a big shot, weren't you?"

"That's not the point," I interrupted him, my body shaking uncontrollably from the waist up. Maybe he sensed something unusual in my voice. He paused a second or two fixing his eyes on me, then he continued:

"To tell you the truth, the whole thing happened because we were told that you had been killed in action. What good will come out of talking about what's gone?

Take it the easy way. If we knew you would be coming back like this, well… but how could we? Maybe all this is luck and destiny, don't you think?"

"But how could Jeong-sun be deceived so easily?" I asked.

"Of course, she remained firm to the end. But maybe Sang-ho knew how to get what he wanted. And I, too, encouraged her to marry him. What else could I do? I thought it would be best to forget you as quickly as possible. I think that's what she thought, too, when she finally decided to marry him."

"All right. I guess that's enough," I said, getting up.

Surprised, he got up, too, saying, "Stay a while longer. Let's have one more drink together and talk."

I didn't stay, but came home.

Sang-ho did not show up until a week passed after I came back. They said he was away on business. When I went to his house, I was told every time that he still was not back. From what I heard at the tavern, he had been seen at the town office where he worked. I did not like to go to the town office, although I did want to find out whether or not he was coming to work.

Presently, a rumor got about that he had not gone away on business, but went to work from his aunt's place in town and occasionally came home stealthily after it got dark.

I was by that time attending the tavern daily at the entrance of our village in the hope of catching up with him. So the rumor reached me quickly.

One day as I was playing *janggi*(Korean chess) in front of the tavern, one of my drinking companions said in a low voice, "Isn't that Sang-ho there?" Turning my head quickly, I saw him riding a bicycle from some distance away toward us.

Putting down the *janggi* piece I was about to move, I went out to the middle of the road to meet him. I was afraid that he would pass by, pretending not to see me. Standing still in the middle of the road, therefore, I raised my hand without a word.

He must have made up his mind to take it if there was no avoiding it. He stopped his bicycle and dismounted.

"Who's this? Isn't this Bong-su?" He shouted as if he were extremely pleased to see me and grabbed me by the hand.

Yes, it's Bong-su, all right—but I did not speak this out loud.

"When did you get back?" He really had been away on a trip, maybe, and was just coming back. But I did not utter the question in so many words.

"So good to see you. Come on in, let's have a drink."

He parked his bicycle outside the tavern and, entering

the place, ordered the proprietress of the tavern to set a table for two.

I did not like the idea of being his guest, but I decided that it was a question of little importance anyway, and let him do as he liked. The attention of all the men in the tavern was at once turned on us. I guessed it was because they all knew how we stood with each other.

"Drink. I have no words to say to you," said Sang-ho, pouring the wine for me.

He had no words to say. What did he mean? Did he mean that he was sorry, or did he mean that he was happy beyond words to see me? There seemed to be no reason why he should be so overjoyed to see me back home that he cannot even find words to express his happy feeling. Of course, we were old friends or we had been anyway, which meant that he had some grounds for pretending to be happy to see me back.

I drank the wine he kept pouring into my bowl. I was still uncomfortable about drinking with him. Reminding myself, however, that it did not matter, I drank on.

How have I been, what part of the country did I fight in mostly, what was this thing they called the Red China's infiltration tactics like, how were the North Koreans, was the food really as bad as they say it was, how were the Americans in battle, wouldn't they after all give us up? etc., etc. He went on and on in this way, and I answered him: well, yes, no, I'm not sure, I don't remember, just so and so, etc. I had already heard that he dodged the draft by bribery. That made me more reluctant to talk about the war with him.

In the meanwhile, we continued to drink. With the rough life I led in the army, it was not likely that I would get easily drunk with a few bowls of thin rice wine, and Sang-ho, as he said himself, seemed to have become a veteran in drinking during the brief while he lived as a town-dweller.

"I would have sent you a letter or two," he said, "had I known where you were. As it was, I could not do so. I am really sorry."

Yes, he was right about his not knowing my address, because we were always moving around. "But what is a letter of sympathy under the circumstances?" I said to myself and emptied another bowl of rice wine.

Not knowing what was in my mind, he continued:

"You know Yeong-suk, don't you, my sister? She is now a senior in high school. She nagged me for your address. I told her I did not know it myself and told her to ask Ok-nan. Ok-nan did not know it, either. Yeong-suk was awfully disappointed."

"Yeong-suk is all right," I said to him in silence. She is better than you. But what does that have to do with our business? Why talk about Yeong-suk while not even mentioning the name of Jeong-sun, who has a dozen times more to do with the two of us?

Gulping down another bowl of wine, I decided that there was no other way to go about it than to bring it up myself.

"Let's talk about Jeong-sun. Tell me briefly what happened." I asked in a soft voice, looking him in the eye.

Sang-ho's head fell as he put his unemptied wine bowl on the table. Then he said with a sigh, "There's not much to say. I am a pig. Forgive me."

I had not expected him to be quite as pliant as this. It occurred to me that alcohol can sometimes work wonders. We grew up in the same village and went to the same elementary and high schools. Therefore we knew each other well. He was financially much better off than I was, but disliked school so much that he did not go to college, though he could well afford it. Instead settled down as a clerk at the town office. As for me, I was an honor student all along and could have obtained a scholarship to some college easily enough. In spite of the intellectual gap between us, I never let go of our friendship, and when he did something that displeased me, I mostly forgave him if he apologized.

Maybe he was relying on this old friendship and his knowledge of my easy-going attitude when he so readily apologized to me that day. Maybe he had counted on getting by with an apology one more time. But if he had, that was a gross miscalculation on his part.

"I won't say many words," I said. "But this is not because I forgive what you have done to me. Things standing as they do, I want to have a talk with you over a certain matter that concerns me seriously."

As if he did not know what to make of my words, he looked up at me with searching eyes.

"What I mean is," I said, "I must see Jeong-sun. I want you to cooperate." Finishing my words, I glared at him with fire in my eyes.

He continued to look at me as if he still did not understand what I meant, and then he lowered his eyes.

"Answer me," I demanded firmly.

He sat for a while,

He raised his eyes slowly to look at me. I could read fear and anxiety on his face.

"What if I say no," he asked in a trembling voice.

"I'll leave that to your imagination. You will see the consequences anyway, so you'll know. But just one word. If you love a comfortable life, you would do well not offending me."

"Is this a threat?" he said, suddenly assuming the posture of a counterattack. I was not a bit ruffled, however. I continued to glare at him without answering.

After a while, I said in a lower tone, "I am not interested at the moment in taking revenge on you in any form. You can take my word for it."

"And then what?" he asked.

"My intention to see Jeong-sun has nothing to do with revenge or resentment. I told you that bygones are bygones. I meant it."

"Then what do you want to see Jeong-sun for?" he asked.

"When I said I would forget what's gone by, I meant what's gone by between you and her, not what's happened between Jeong-sun and me; that is my past, or rather our past. Since I have given my word to keep a certain agreement between us, you see, it's my duty to see her as long as she is living."

"Do you mean," he said, "even if she is now another man's wife and has a child by him?"

"Of course," I pursued, "whether she is another man's wife, or whether she's another man's slave, I don't care. I am going to ignore everything that has happened while I was away."

At this point, I noticed that Sang-ho appeared to be trying very hard, on his own part, to find the right answer to the problem he was faced with. Then, he said, "Aren't you ignoring reality a little too much?" His tone was more plaintive than offended.

"Reality?" I said, "Oh, yes, that's it. You have never gone to war. That's why you talk about reality. Look! This is reality, do you see?" I put my right hand before him. It was an ugly, reddish brown hand with second and third fingers missing.

"You remember my hand before I went into the army. Now, is this reality or dream?" I asked.

"Oh," he exclaimed, "I noticed that there was something wrong with your hand. You've lost two fingers. It's too bad."

"You now talk about my fingers. But I am talking about reality. What two fingers? They don't matter. But reality does, don't you think? If I had known Jeong-sun was already married, I would not have come back brandishing this ugly hand... You still think I'm talking about my fingers, but that's not true. I am talking about my life which I have brought back by mistake. There is the reason why I have to see Jeong-sun. Now that I am back with this ugly hand, I simply must see her. Let me hear your answer now."

"If that's how you feel," he said, "Let me think this over until tomorrow. As you must know, it's not a matter I can decide alone. I will have to ask her first, and then my parents too, because I don't think I ought to decide such a matter without consulting my parents. You understand, don't you?"

I felt disgusted and impatient with what he said and his manner of saying it, but I managed to restrain myself. I thought this was no time to argue with him. I said:

"Let me hear from you by this hour tomorrow. Let me know where and when I can see her," I spat out the words and got up.

The next evening, Yeong-suk came with a note from him. It read:

"I am sorry about yesterday. I hope to be forgiven by you. I would like to invite you to dinner at our place. I very much want you to come. Affectionately, Sang-ho."

Yeong-suk was sitting on the edge of the *toenmaru*[1] while she waited for me to finish reading the letter. But then she got up and said:

"My brother told me to be sure to bring you along with me." She smiled prettily.

"Wait," I said and called Ok-nan for a piece of paper and a pencil. I wrote: "I am sorry I cannot accept your invitation. As I said yesterday, I must see Jeong-sun. Let me know before noon tomorrow where and when I can see her. If Jeong-sun wishes it, she may be accompanied by Yeong-suk."

Yeong-suk took the slip of paper I handed her and,

---

1 A narrow wooden terrace protruding from the outer wall of a room in traditional Korean housing.

bowing to me politely, went away.

It was not until the next evening that Yeong-suk appeared with another letter. She said she had been told to bring it to me within the morning hours, but could not come earlier because she got back from school late. I could not tell whether she was making up the story or not.

The handwriting in the slip was the same as the last. "Thank you for answering. I must let you know that my wife is scheduled to pay a visit to her family in the near future, accompanied by Yeong-suk. Through my sister you will learn when it will be."

Two days after was Sunday. Yeong-suk came and told Ok-nan that she and Jeong-sun were going to see Jeong-sun's people. She did not want to tell me directly. I did not ask her questions, either. Instead, I told Ok-nan afterward that I would like her to watch out for them and let me know instantly if she saw them leave their house for their trip to Owl's Corner. Then I went to the barbershop and had my first haircut in a long time.

Just as the barber finished giving me a shave after the haircut, Ok-nan came to tell me of their departure. I started for Owl's Corner where Jeong-sun's old home was. It was late in the afternoon when I got there.

As I walked into their yard, Yeong-suk seemed to be

admiring the peony plants growing by the *Jangttokdae*[2] touching a blossom with her fingertips. She nodded to me when her eyes caught me, then she ran toward the Lower Room.[3] She disappeared into the room, closing the door after her. "She is showing me where Jeong-sun is," I thought, and waited.

Finally, the door of the room slid open and I saw the sad, lotus face of Jeong-sun that I had dreamed of, oh, for so many nights. I could not tell you what clothes she wore or what change had occurred to her person. All I was conscious of was her being there. There was the sad lotus face of my girl right before me. I felt only quick throbs in my heart and turmoil in my blood stream. I even forgot to offer greetings to the other people in the house. I merely stood there in front of the room as if frozen to the ground.

Jeong-sun presently stood up in the room but, lowering her head, remained wordless. Yeong-suk stood up too, but did not smile. She looked different as she stood there in silence, without smiling and without her usual friendliness.

I knew I could not expect a "Come in" from either of them, so I entered the room of my own accord, taking off my shoes.

---

2 An open terrace where earthenware jars are kept.
3 A usually small-size room separated from the main quarter by a yard.

Even after I entered the room and seated myself, the two of them were still standing with their eyes lowered.

In fact, I was too preoccupied to be concerned about whether they were standing or seated. I held my head lower than theirs because I had to hide the tears which welled up in my eyes. My shoulders shook in spite of my effort not to cry.

When at last I could bring myself to raise my head, I saw that they were now seated. "This is certainly no dream. I am seeing Jeong-sun. I still see her sitting in front of me. Yes, it's Jeong-sun. I have nothing to regret now,"—such thoughts raced on in my head....

Then, I came to myself recovering a measure of composure. I raised my eyes and looked straight at Jeong-sun for the first time. I could not see her full in the face yet, but I could at least look at her forehead.

"Jeong-sun," I called in a trembling voice.

"Maybe this is going to be the last time I call you like this, but allow me this once to address you like in the old days. You too, Yeong-suk, forgive me."

As I said this, I felt another lump welling up in my throat. I clenched my teeth in order to keep the lump down. But the effort only hurt my throat enormously, and the lump there continued to push its way up toward my eyes where it turned into hot liquid. The hot liquid flowed out of my eyes, but I thought it was at least better than sobbing because it was less obtrusive. I took out my handkerchief and wiped the tears, then spoke again:

"It must be as painful for you as it is for me, I mean, having to watch me cry. But I did not mean to show you my tears when I said I wanted to see you. Just ignore them. They will be over soon."

I lit a cigarette and slowly exhaled the smoke a couple of times. Then I said:

"Things are rather different from what I imagined out there fighting. If I had known it would be like this, I probably would not have taken the actions that I have. No, there would have been no need for that. But, I will try to give as little pain to you or Yeong-suk as possible, so I will make my story short." After this preface, I held out my right hand before them, and said, "Look, this is my hand. Two fingers gone. Thanks to them, I was discharged from the army, because one cannot shoot with a hand like this. But believe me, I am not telling you this because I think there is anything in this that one can boast of. There are men who lost both arms, both legs, their eyes their nose, or ears. Yes, this really is nothing compared with what they lost. Or with those who lost their lives."

I went on after a pause: "But it is after all because of this maimed hand that I have regrets. I did not get this from the enemy. This was my own doing. I did this to save my life. Yes, I wanted to keep at least my life."

As I talked on, I was overcome by an uncontrollable surge of emotion. I lit another cigarette and for a long while sat silent looking down.

Jeong-sun and Yeong-suk had now grown bold enough to raise their heads to look at me now and then.

I puffed out another wreath of smoke and continued:

"I was with a reconnaissance squad. You probably don't know what that is. It moves into enemy lines ahead of the rest of the other troops. In the reconnaissance squad, you are never sure whether you are really alive or dead. Once out on a mission, the chances that you'd return alive are less than fifty percent. Such missions often left half of us dead. Of course, it was not infrequent that a wholesale slaughter happened, only one or two surviving.

"We are supposed to serve only a brief term and then get transferred to a softer job, but only in theory. Experienced soldiers are scarce, so it is not easy to get a transfer. I was worse off than most. They said I was smart, experienced, and what not, and wouldn't let me go. They called me 'invulnerable,' because I always returned alive to the headquarters even when almost everybody else got killed.

"To make the long story short, while all this was going on, I had only one thought, that I could not die while my Jeong-sun was still living. I had no right to die, I said to myself. Maybe the secret of my invulnerable life, too, lay in my thoughts of you. Yet I also knew that there was a limit to human will and luck. One day I would not be able to escape but would die, and they were not going to give me a transfer.

"I finally made a resolution; I resolved not to die. I decided to do something about my fate which might turn against me at any moment. No, Jeong-sun, it was not that I was afraid of death. I saw enough deaths about me, the mangled bodies of so many of my comrades. No, I wasn't exactly a coward. One can die from patriotism, righteousness, humanism, or whatever else is there to bolster up one's strength.

"I did not myself have much of those grand sentiments. Yet I would have gladly died for the sake of being freed from the pain and remorse the war made me know. Yes, I ought to have been dead, Jeong-sun. But I chose to live. And it was because of my thoughts of you."

I paused.

Jeong-sun had been crying for some time with her face turned towards the wall. Yeong-suk left the room with her handkerchief at her eyes.

"But now," I resumed, "what do I find? I've come back only to find you a married woman. I do not blame you or anybody else for that. I heard that Sang-ho got you by deception."

"Oh, no," Jeong-sun said, "I was to blame. I was a fool. I ought to have died." Jeong-sun now began to cry audibly.

"The question is," I said, "that my real problem begins now. What should I do with myself now? I no longer have any use for my life, which, yes, I have stolen dishonorably. I cannot go on living this stolen life. I shan't be forgiven. Not only because I sinned against my country, but because I betrayed those wretched, heroic suffering men who were my comrades."

"The cross of a traitor is not the hate and anger of others, but his own loneliness. If I knew that there was no longer the Jeong-sun of my memory, I would have died a dozen deaths at the front than come back like this. I should have stuck with them and died with them. Death is nothing to be feared at the front. I always envied the war dead their rest. Now what shall I do with this superfluous life hanging heavy on my hands?"

"Please kill me!" said Jeong-sun.

Now she was hitting her forehead against the wall. And her body was trembling all over.

"Listen, Jeong-sun," I said, "I will consider what passed between you and Sang-ho as something that has never happened. I said the same thing to Sang-ho. If only you come back to me, I will forget whatever happened in my absence. Jeong-sun, leave him and come to me. We will get married. If you don't like to live on in this village, we can go to some other place. I am ready to forsake my mother and sister as I did my comrades at the front."

"But would they let me go?" said Jeong-sun in a low voice, as if she were merely talking to herself.

"I stole my life and came back only out of my determination to be near you. Now things depend on your determination. As you must see yourself, there is no other way. Do as I told you, and give me back my life. I have this life in order to be with you. Otherwise, it is the life of a dirty traitor. It's something one would fear to carry on one's back. Something that should be cast away. I mean it. You'll see."

"I am so scared," said Jeong-sun. Her chin was trembling.

"Why should you be scared? If you married Sang-ho for love or if you love him now, I wouldn't insist. If not, it would be only right for you to give my life some justification for its preservation. It would be right, not wrong for us to be happy together. You understand this, don't you? Please, answer me."

Instead of an answer, Jeong-sun nodded her head once. Just then, the door of the room slid open, and Yeong-suk came in.

"Excuse me, but…" she said hesitantly, then drew our attention to the open door by turning her head that way. There we saw Jeong-sun's sister-in-law standing in the doorway holding a tray in her hands.

Jeong-sun's sister-in law said, "I fixed some noodles for you. Please help yourself. And you, *agassi*,[4] won't you come in and eat with us inside?" Then she placed the tray over the threshold on the doorside floor of the room. Jeong-sun, in turn, took up the tray and placed in front of me.

She said softly, "Help yourself. As for what you said, I will do what I can." She left the room to join the women in another room.

I did not eat the noodles. Lighting a cigarette and, putting on my shoes, I left the room and walked out of the house.

I did not hear from Jeong-sun for some time. It wouldn't be easy for a married woman with a child to leave her home, I thought. But I could not sit still, just waiting. I wrote a letter addressed to her (*I know there must be difficulties. You have your child and your own people to think of, besides your husband and your parents-in-law. Yet do not forget that this is a matter of life and death*). "Please hurry." I handed the letter to Ok-nan, saying, "Give this to Jeong-sun, but don't let others

---

4 Younger sister-in-law, also, any young woman.

see you. Maybe, you could ask Yeong-suk to do it?"

"It won't be easy," said Ok-nan "These days Jeong-sun doesn't even come out to the well often. And, as for Yeong-suk, she certainly is very fond of you, but can we really expect her to care for you more than she cares for her own brother?" All the same, Ok-nan folded the letter and hid it in her bosom.

As she had forewarned, Ok-nan did not succeed in catching Jeong-sun in private, but at least she seemed to see Yeong-suk now and then.

"Couldn't you get Yeong-suk to tell you anything?" I asked Ok-nan, one day.

"She says she is sad these days," Ok-nan said.

"Why?"

"She was there with you and Jeong-sun that day, wasn't she? She says she doesn't know who she should side with. She is just so very sad, she says."

"She has nothing to do with it. Why should she care?"

"It isn't quite that simple. She is a very sensitive girl. She has read many books. Won't you talk to her yourself? She may be willing to help you if you asked her in person."

I did not say anything.

Five days had passed since I had left the message with Ok-nan. Then, on the sixth evening, right after supper, Yeong-suk came with a letter from Jeong-sun. The letter said: "They have found out about my plan. I am in a terrible situation now. I don't intend to give up my promise with you for good. I swear that I will carry it out one day as long as you wait for me. For the present, consider me a rotten whore. Mine is a wretched, miserable life that drags on simply because I don't have courage. Do forgive me and don't be too impatient. Yours, Jeong-sun."

I read the letter twice. Not that there was anything hard to understand in the letter. Only I seemed to read her destiny on that slip of paper. Jeong-sun was like this always: good, wise, affectionate and faithful. But she never was a strong woman. She was soft. She was malleable to external circumstances. Of course, she is not even now deceiving me or herself. She is only accommodating herself to the environment. Rather than her will, her external circumstances will always rule her.

Crumpling up the letter, I put it into my pocket and, turning to Yeong-suk, asked her: "Who wrote that letter you just gave me?"

"My sister-in-law," she answered, blushing a little.

"You know what's written in it, too, don't you?"

She blushed again and did not answer.

"I trust you as much as I do Ok-nan. Please answer my question. You know, don't you?"

Ok-nan answered for her by nodding her head once.

"Be a good friend to Ok-nan even after I am gone," I said to Yeong-suk not quite knowing myself what I meant by that. Then, I left the house hurriedly.

Maybe I had thought of going away, it wouldn't matter where. I may have just wanted to hide myself somewhere. I certainly could not lie in the room not doing anything. Maybe I thought it would be better to end my life than wait for her without hope or keep on reproaching her.

I walked around to the backside of my house. From there to the foot of the mountain that marked the horizon stretched a great expanse of barley fields. I could smell the barley ripening in fat ears as I walked along the path between the barley fields as if in a trance. Then, I seemed to hear somebody's footsteps behind me. But I was too tired and indifferent to look back. I continued to walk. Maybe I was going to walk and walk like that until I fell to the ground exhausted.

Dusk was descending over the barley fields.

Birds—maybe pigeons, maybe some other kind of birds—were flying in the darkening sky, looking like a bunch of tiny black pebbles.

Suddenly it occurred to me that I could be walking in a dream. I stopped and dazedly looked up into the sky toward where the pebble-like black objects had flown away... And it was then that I heard her voice: "*Oppa!*"

Her voice was so low that I could have easily missed it. It was Yeong-suk. I stared into her face with vacant eyes for a long time. "Do you mean you are sad too? Are you saying you wish to share my grief?" I asked in my mind, still dazed.

Yeong-suk stood, motionless, like myself. (*Please don't kill yourself, brother. I will give you my love. I will do anything for you, if only I can assuage your grief.*) These words seemed to be forming in her closed mouth.

Next moment, she was in my arms. To be more exact, I first drew her to me by the wrist, and she threw herself into my arms.

But now I don't know how to justify my subsequent act. I have no way to explain how I came to feel such an impulsive lust or why she did not try to defend herself from me who was by then no more than a wild beast.

Anyway, with Yeong-suk still in my arms, I ducked into a barley field and, tearing off her thin clothing, began to defile her innocent body. Whether it was from despair, fear, or resignation, I could not tell, but Yeong-suk offered little resistance to my rough hands. She could have been unconscious, of course. But, it is more likely that she was offering her entire self, including her life, in payment for my loss and for my tears.

Just then I heard the cawing of the magpies—the same magpies that started my mother's coughing. At the same moment, something like a powerful electric wave began to course through my entire body—my limbs, my heart, my brain, and even the tips of my hair.

The magpies cawed again. This time, the sound seemed to come from inside of me as well. Slowly, I lowered my hands onto her chest as if I were about to raise the body of the girl who lay there half unconscious. The next moment, my two hands were pressing her tender neck down against the ground.

Deungsin-bul[1]

Deungsin-bul is the name given to the Buddha enshrined in Geumbul-gak(Shrine of the Golden Buddha) at Jeongwon-sa, a temple to the north of the Yangtze River. This statue of Buddha is also called Deungsin Geumbul or just Geumbul(the Golden Buddha).

What I intend to do here is to write down what I have seen and heard of this Deungsin-bul or Deungsin Geumbul. But first, I would like to tell my readers how I came to visit this Buddhist temple, Jeongwon-sa, which was in such a faraway location, a foreign country to boot.

I was twenty-two years old and was attending Taisho Daigaku[2] in Japan when I was drafted as a so-called 'student soldier' to fight in the Japanese Army. It was in

---

[1] A Buddha statue of human size by common usage but here used to mean the particular Buddha statue in China that the story depicts.
[2] A buddhist college in the Tokyo area.

the early summer of 1943.

The detachment to which I was allocated went to Peking and from there to Nanking by way of Soochow. We were supposed to stay in that city until another detachment arrived.

However, as our period of waiting was prolonged, our status in the city became more like that of a garrison than that of troops on a temporary stay. In the meantime, we were actually performing various duties of a garrison.

Although vaguely, we knew that when we were moved out of Nanking, we were going to be sent to either Indochina or Indonesia. Therefore, few of us regretted the delay in the arrival of another detachment to relieve us from our garrison duties. Rather, most of us harbored a wish that we be detained in Nanking as long as possible because it meant keeping ourselves alive that much longer.

In my case, it was not just wishful thinking. On the contrary, I was determined that I would try whatever method available to save myself before the detachment should be transferred out of Nanking. In fact, I had done some "research" in order to materialize this plan in case a proper opportunity should present itself. My research work consisted of making a list of Chinese Buddhist scholars who had studied in Japan(especially those who studied at Taisho Daigaku). When I found the name "Jin Gi-su" given as a resident of Nanking on a sheet of secret documents, I was so excited that I nearly felt faint.

However, it was not easy for a Korean soldier belonging to the Japanese Army to look up a man in a foreign city. If finding him had not been a matter of life and death for me, and if the image of the Merciful Goddess had not smiled down at me constantly I would not have found the courage and wisdom to go through with it. And it was at this critical moment that I learned from a monk who belonged to a Buddhist missionary corps that Mr. Jin Gi-su was at the moment residing in a hermitage in complete solitude. The name of the hermitage, I was told, was Seogong-am.

The city of Nanking was getting dark when I paid a visit to Mr. Jin Gi-su at his hermitage. I folded my hands in *hapjang*[3] as soon as I saw him and kotowed many times to show my deep respect for him and also to let him see the urgency of my need to see him. After this preliminary ceremony, I told him my circumstances as well as I could.

But, from his point of view, I was not only an utter stranger, but a soldier belonging to the enemy camp. I saw that his eyebrows were knitted in an expression of displeasure. But just as words of refusal to my entreaty

---

3 Buddhist practice of folding hands in greeting or in a pray.

were about to fall from his mouth(or at least I thought they were), I took out the white sheet of paper I had prepared beforehand and, biting a morsel of flesh off my index finger, wrote with the blood that flowed out of the wound: Wonmyeon Salsaeng Kwi-euibuleun(願免殺生 歸依佛恩), which meant that I wanted to be exempted from the offence of life-taking and to reside in the merciful world of Buddha forever.

I offered these eight characters written in blood to him and again folded my hands in *hapjang*.

I saw what seemed to be a change in the expression on Mr. Jin Gi-su's face. The expression I saw now was not exactly that of delight or satisfaction but at least it was devoid of the firm air of refusal it had before.

After a brief silence, Mr. Jin Gi-su said:

"Follow me."

I got up at once and hurried after him.

It was a small room in the innermost part of the building that Mr. Jin Gi-su took me to. He left me in this room and walked away again closing the door after him. After a while, however, he came back with a suit of monk's clothes and said:

"Change into these."

After these words, he left the room again closing the door after him.

I breathed a long sigh of relief. For the first time, I felt that now I would be able to live.

When I changed into the monk's clothes, I was given a simple supper on a tray which was pushed into the room. I took the tray without a word and ate up everything on it quickly.

As soon as I pushed the tray back into the hall outside the room, Mr. Jin Gi-su came in with an old monk as if they had been waiting right outside my room while I ate.

"Go with him," he said. "I gave my letter of introduction to him. The letter is addressed to the father monk of the main temple."

I did not venture to say anything but merely bowed my head again and again in complete obeisance. What else could I do when he was the only one in the whole wide world who could save my life? I entrusted myself to him entirely.

"The road which you will take is not known to the Japanese soldiers. It's a mountain path about one hundred *li*(40kilometers) from here. Today is the twenty-first, however, and there will be some moonlight later on, I believe. Well, then, I pray that Buddha's protection be with you. Namu-gwanse-eumbosal.⁴"

Mr. Jin Gi-su folded his hands and bowed to me. I could not find a word to say to him. My throat choked and tears welled up in my eyes. In this state, I folded my

---

4 A Buddhist invocation.

hands and bowed back to him.

Gyeong-am—the old monk who was my guide—walked fast in spite of the darkness and unevenness of the road. No doubt he was accustomed to this mountain route. Even so, it was a journey filled with so many perils. Fallen branches of trees seemed to be lying in wait to catch the night-travelers' feet ever so often and there were hollow spots where the earth had sunken. Jagged tips of buried rocks presented a further hurdle while the path was even crossed by slippery mud streams that were deftly hidden by the overgrown grass. But all these impediments were nothing to the old monk, apparently. He walked just as easily as if he were walking on an open smooth road. The only advantage I had over him was that I was much younger than he was. I soon realized, however, that he was not going to allow me even this one upper hand. Because even after a nonstop walk of thirty *li*, he was still not tired and did not suggest a break.

I struggled after him as best I could, constantly wiping away the sweat that broke out on my forehead. Still, more often than not, I lost him in the darkness and was driven to a panic. I got my face scratched by the branches of the trees more than a couple of times and hurt my knees by falling over the protruding rocks. And all of this naturally put a further distance between me and the old monk. Many times, I called out to him: "*Daesa!*" Gyeong-am would stop when he was called and, mumbling something, would wait for me to catch up. But the minute I appeared within sight, he would turn about and walk on as swiftly as before.

It was long after midnight when the crescent moon appeared in the sky and began to light up our road with its dim illumination. I was immensely relieved by this and from then on could walk after Gyeong-am with more ease and speed. Now I will never lose sight of him, I said to myself, no matter how fast he walks!

Maybe the old monk sensed the change in our situation. When I came up to him, he turned to look at me and, stretching one arm toward a distant sky, drew a semicircle in the air. He said "Two hundred *li*." I guessed what he meant to say was that if we had taken the smooth good road to the temple instead of this steep short-cut, the journey would have amounted to two hundred *li*.

I repeated "yes, yes,"(about the only Chinese word I knew how to pronounce) and nodded my head vigorously.

It was late next morning that we arrived in front of the outer gate of the Jeongwon-sa Temple. Gyeong-am pointed to the tile-roofed buildings that showed between the trees and said something I could not understand. I noticed that his face beamed with pride as he pointed out the dark-tiled buildings to me. I nodded my head again heartily and said: "Good! Good!"

We walked through the outer gate and then through the main gate. Suddenly, I was faced with a tremendously huge garret that loomed in the front. The signboard said *Taeheoru*.

We went round the *Taeheoru* and went into the inner courtyard. Right on the opposite side of the courtyard from the entrance loomed an outstandingly large-sized building which I gathered to be the main hall of worship. But what were the functions of all the minor buildings that lay sideways, lengthwise, high-up or low-down adjacent to the main building, I wondered bewilderedly but utterly overcome by the majesty of it all.

Gyeong-am led me through many an alley between these buildings and finally stopped in front of a little house with a signboard that said: *Cheongjeongsil*. As he made a coughing signal, the door in the front of the house opened, and a young monk about the age of twenty poked his head out. He made a greeting sign to Gyeong-am. The two of them, the young monk standing in the doorway and the old monk standing outside the door, conversed for some time. Finally, Gyeong-am motioned me to follow him into the house.

A tall, old man with completely white hair greeted us

with a smile as we entered the room. Since I did not know any Chinese except a couple of words, I contented myself with folding my hands and bowing to him very politely.

The white-haired monk was smiling and nodding his head. He then opened the letter from Mr. Jin Gi-su handed to him by Gyeong-am, who had in the meantime designated me a place to sit down.

"This is the blessing of Buddha," said the elder monk after reading the letter from Mr. Jin Gi-su. I did not understand what he said at the time but found out the meaning of his words later on when my understanding of Chinese improved. Later, I also found out that this white-haired, old monk was the very person Mr. Jin Gi-su had called "the father monk," that his proper sacred name was Wonhye Daesa and that he had been the head monk of this temple until two years ago.

That night, I slept in a small room next to Cheongjeongsil where the old master resided. The young monk who led me to my new abode—he was something of a secretary to the old master—said, "I am your neighbor," and grinned widely. He said he was called Cheong-un.

Although I was thus allotted a separate room and a kind of independence, I did not spend my time idling. I did not wish to betray the trust and goodness Mr. Jin Gi-su—his sacred name was Hyeun—and Wonhye Daesa showed me. I made up my mind that I would not behave in such a way as would bring disgrace on either of them.

Consequently, I was up and around at the earliest possible hour, washing myself, offering early morning prayers, and cleaning, along with Cheong-un, the halls, corridors and every other space in and out of the Cheongjeongsil.

I also followed after the monks when they went to collect herbs for medicine and food. (As everywhere else in this war period, food was getting scarce in this temple and so the monks went around the mountains to gather edible plants and roots.)

After work, I came back to my room with my hands and feet washed up and either read the Buddhist scriptures or learned Chinese from Cheong-un. This project was more successful than I had expected, and after only a few days' studying, I could exchange some simple words with my teacher although they were only very rudimentary in content.

I tried not to lie down or rest in any sloppy way even if I was in my room by myself until it became time for me to sleep at night. I really put in a lot of effort to accomplish this. When I felt so sleepy that I could not sit up straight, I went out of my room and walked about so as not to lie down before bedtime.

When I roamed out of my abode in this way, I did not at first know where to go. But I soon stopped roaming. It was because I found a destination. It was a shrine called the Geumbul-gak (The shrine of Golden Buddha).

I looked at the hall of worship first. I did not do this necessarily because of the fact that the main hall of a temple where the principal image of Buddha is housed usually offered the best introduction to the general tenor and standing of a Buddhist temple. Rather, I chose to look at it first because that had become a habit with me as with many other people beginning a tour of a temple or a shrine from its main hall. My inspection of the main hall, however, assured me that there was nothing very special about it compared with the main halls of the temples or shrines I had seen in Korea or Japan up to that time. It may be that it had thicker pillars or larger-sized images, but the differences, if there were any, were negligible. The coloring and the engraving, too, were not any more sophisticated or artistically executed than in main halls of other worshipping places I had seen. If I were pressed to point out any notable characteristic of this place, I might say that the three gilt statues of Buddha raised up high in the center of the altar looked as if they might have come out as winners in a contest of strength with the other statues I had seen elsewhere. That is, the Buddhas in this shrine looked physically stronger than the Buddhas of other places. However, this was entirely my own subjective impression of the place. To those who worshiped here, what appeared to me as their superior physical strength must have felt like so much more saintliness.

To be more precise, it was only after I happened to take a look at the Golden statue of Buddha in the Shrine of Golden Buddha that I began to associate the three Buddhas in the main hall of worship with saintliness or spiritual power. Because the sight of the Golden Buddha seemed gradually to throw a new light of holiness over everything I saw in the place including the three Buddhas.

I had not heard from either Cheong-un or Wonhye Daesa about the Shrine of Golden Buddha. Even so, I was not without the feeling that there was something peculiar about this shrine. For one thing, it was constructed and situated in an unexpected manner. It was built at the back of the main hall on a stone terrace of about fifty square meters on an elevated terrain which could be reached from the road by climbing a set of stone steps. To reach the shrine, one had to walk on the stone terrace quite some length, which meant that the stone terrace formed a sort of a gateway to the shrine. The stone slabs forming the terrace were square in shape and were covered with dark-green moss. To have an overall picture of the shrine, one needs only to imagine a structure built on a hill elaborately clothed with elegantly cut stone slabs in the general direction of northeast at the back of the main hall. The eaves were gilded all around and so was the signboard hanging in front of the shrine. The engravings and the paintings on the outer walls of the shrine, too, were richly gilded. Therefore, looking from the outside, the whole building seemed to glow in heavy gold.

I had never liked gilded things whether fabric, paper, wood or metal. I felt some antipathy, therefore, when first laying my eyes on the golden-ornamented Geumbul-gak, or the Shrine of Golden Buddha. It was undeniable, however, that to those who built it and those who worshipped there, the place must have a very special meaning. So much elaborate decorating could not have been done without a very special and deep feeling of adoration and, probably, a genuine affection, I thought.

In my mind, however, I decided that whatever it was that the people so adored, valued and guarded in such a special manner inside the shrine could not amount to anything much. My past experience had taught me that this sort of a thing in a Buddhist temple usually housed some statue of Buddha gilded with a pile of gold bestowed by a king or an emperor. Or it could be a statue built by some emperor in memory of his dead queen. In either case, it was no more than a conspicuous show of power.

My conviction about the golden statue grew firmer as the other monks refused to open the door of the shrine to me. I was told that unless one brought five silver pieces as an offering, the door would not be opened. Another occasion when the door opened was when there were prayers on behalf of some important personages. But even at these times, unless one was a monk belonging to Jeongwon-sa, one had to offer money to be allowed into the shrine.

As I learned more about it, my conviction that Geumbul-gak was nothing more than a gimmick was fortified. It must be something invented merely to draw money out of the pockets of the believers, I decided.

When Cheong-un came to my room to teach me Chinese, however, I asked him all the same, affecting non-chalance:

"What is Geumbul-gak, I mean, that thing over there?"

"Why do you ask?"

Cheong-un asked back with a meaningful smile.

"They would not open the door for me to take a look."

"Shall we go back now and try again?"

"No, I will try another time...."

"It will be the same even then. Come on. Let's go and see what happens while your mind is bent that way."

As if to oblige Cheong-un, who seemed to rather wish me to do it, I got up and followed him out.

As if to dispense with any possible complications, Cheong-un went straight to the old monk in charge of the shrine and borrowed the key to the shrine from him. Opening the door of the shrine with key, Chong-un stood deferentially with folded hands.

As for me, I was, with opening the door, thrown into such a bizarre state of shock that I even forgot to fold my hands or bow my head. The first thing I recorded mentally was the fact that the statue was indeed thickly plated with gold, just as I had expected. My anticipation proved wrong on all other points apart from one aspect, however. The statue of Buddha was very different from the picture I had had in my mind before I saw it. First of all, it had an incense-burner on its head. His hands were folded reverently in the front, but his mouth was half opened in a sloppy manner. What I was seeing was not the usual image of dignity, holiness and physical perfection at all. In short, the Buddha I saw was exceedingly shabby-looking. In addition, there was something about this Buddha that filled one's heart with a nearly insufferable sense of pain. It was a life-size statue in the formal Gyeolgabujwa[5] posture. As I looked on, I was more and more astounded that the image I saw before my eyes was so immeasurably different from the usual saintly, dignified and beautiful Buddha image one might find in such a gilded shrine standing on an elegant stone terrace. What a pitiful-looking, heartrending Buddha image it was! The sitting Buddha could not even sit straight! And the expression on the face above which sat the incense-burner was like nothing I could think of. For one moment, it was that of a man crying, then, that of a man laughing. When one looked again, the face was grimacing, and then it looked as if it were agonizing in indescribable sorrow and pain. As I looked on, I began to feel something choking me in the chest as if to smother me. It was a sitting statue of Buddha I had never once seen or heard of.

I said I was shocked by my first sight of the statue. But it is impossible for me to describe what exactly it was that shocked me. I only remember the fact that as I kept looking at the statue, the feeling of shock changed itself gradually into a feeling of fear and that I ended up feeling all shaken up as if something powerful had given me a violent beating. When Cheong-un turned his head to me, I was frozen in a state of complete immovability with only the lower halves of my legs and my chin trembling as if in a fit. *That is no Buddha! That is no statue*

---

5 Sitting in a formal style of Buddhist tradition.

of Buddha! Without knowing it, I was feverishly yearning to shout these words at the top of my voice. My throat was blocked up, however, and I could produce no sound.

When I showed up in front of Wonhye Daesa after the morning prayers with Cheong-un the next day, the Master asked:

"Did you go to the Geumbul-gak yesterday?"

When I answered in a fearful voice that I did indeed worship at the shrine, he said contentedly:

"It's Buddha's blessing."

I wanted to shout: It was no Buddha! He did not have the Buddha's face!

But I kept my mouth shut.

But the Master seemed to know what was in my mind. He said:

"Which Buddha did you like best?"

The fact was that, driven out of my wits at the sight of the golden statue, I had not had a chance to look at the other Buddhas in the shrine.

"I did not see other Buddhas. The Buddha in the center frightened me so much that I…"

At this point, my lower chin started trembling again, and I could not continue with my words.

Wonhye Taesa looked at my face, my chin still trembling. Suddenly I remembered that I had just uttered the word Buddha referring to the fearful ugly statue. So I hurried to say as if I had uttered something I had no right to:

"But no… no… it was not… it was not the face of a Buddha."

I said this, summoning up all the strength that lay in me.

"Why? Is it because he has the incense-burner on his head instead of a wreath? It is really an incense-burner that he has on his head, isn't it?"

He did not sound reproachful. On the contrary, he seemed to be rather favorably interested in my reaction. I did not say anything further. Instead I stared into the Master's eyes steadily for so long that Cheong-un gave me a warning sign with his eyes a couple of times.

"According to you, maybe, he is no Buddha but a *Nahan*,[6] is that what you think? But even a *Nahan* does not hold an incense-burner on his head. Not even among all the Five-Hundred-*Nahan*s is there any with an incense-burner on the head.…"

I kept my silence and continued to stare at the Master, my mind bursting with wonder and curiosity.

But he did not seem inclined to go on.

"In a way, you are right. He was not a Buddha origi-nally. It is just that everybody came to call him Buddha.

---

6 Buddha's disciple.

He was the father monk of this temple. Since he attained Buddhahood, however, everybody began to call him Buddha. You will, too."

After these words, the Master folded his hands together. I too folded my hands in *hapjang*, bowing my head at the same time and got up from my seat.

As I was returning to my room after the morning service, Cheong-un caught up with me. Pointing toward Geumbul-gak with his chin, he said:

"I was puzzled at first just like you. But he is the Buddha that has worked more miracles than any other Buddha in this temple."

"Miracles?" I said as if surprised by the word. But in fact I was more surprised that Cheong-un called the statue "Buddha" without any inhibition whatsoever. Although it was only a while ago that Wonhye Daesa had told me that "everybody began to call him Buddha," I found myself not ready to accept the appellation as yet. Maybe the fixed idea about what a Buddha should look like was too firmly implanted in my head for me to even begin considering the ungainly statue a Buddha... I could not take a monk for a Buddha, in any case!

"Yes, miracles. That is why there's so much money offered at his shrine," Cheong-un said. And he continued:

"Nobody knew the real name of the monk. He lived

during the Dang dynasty, one thousand and several hundred years ago. He attained Buddhahood by (*sosin gongyang*), that is, by burning himself in offering. While the process of his self-offering devotion continued, many a miracle occurred. People who saw, or heard of, these miracles thronged to the temple and offered money and prayers. None among them went home without receiving some miracle. The miracles happened afterward, too, and the number of people who were given a child or had their sickness cured by praying at the shrine was uncountable. There were thousands of other people who had wishes other than these fulfilled...."

When I heard the word *sosin gongyang* from Cheong-un's mouth, a shiver went through my body.

"That explains..." I said not fully realizing what I meant by these words. I closed my eyes and folded my hands in *hapjang*. "Namuamitabul, namuamitabul," my lips mumbled on by themselves.

Oh that he should have gone through so much suffering and sorrow! The tears oozed out of my closed eyes. "Namuamitabul, namuamitabul," I repeated impulsively.

"I too felt like crying at first. But as I kept on seeing him, I became more used to the Buddha." Cheong-un said with a smile as if to comfort me.

There was, however, still one point which was not

clear to me. It was that if he had attained the Buddhahood through *sosin gongyang*, shouldn't he look like a Buddha? Shouldn't he be the image of holiness, harmony and peace? Even if he could not exactly fit into this mould, shouldn't he at least come close to it? But there was nothing holy, harmonious or peaceful about the sitting statue. It had too much of human agony and sorrow on the face. Then why is it that this particular Buddha works more wonders than many a holy man in the past who attained Buddhahood?

These questions stayed in my head and would not go away. Besides, after hearing about the way in which the monk had offered himself, that is, by *sosin gongyang*, I kept seeing the Buddha as a huge chunk of burnt coal.

Three days later I visited the golden statue again. I had come to think that maybe, on my previous visit, my mind was not in a proper, lucid state but was inclined to a morbid fantasizing and that was why I experienced that kind of a benumbing shock. Maybe, as Cheong-un suggested, if I looked at the Buddha again, I might become less affected by its appearance, I said to myself, maybe I will be able to cope with the sense of pain and sorrow so agonizingly emitted by the sitting Buddha....

When the door opened, I bowed my head and folded my hands as I had seen Cheong-un do the first day. My mouth uttered the invocation, "Namuamitabul" repeatedly.

When finally I opened my eyes and looked at the Buddha, I found him sitting, like before, with the incense-burner on his head and in the same deep sorrow and suffering in which I had found him previously. Again, I could not find a trace of holiness or peace about him. Unlike on the previous occasion, however, I did not experience the acute sadness or feeling of pity for the Buddha this time. Maybe it was because my mind was already desensitized with anticipation of sadness so that I had stopped expecting from him the usual attributes of a Buddha: holiness harmony and peace.

I closed my eyes again and, folding my hands, repeated "Namuamitabul" until my lips trembled from exhaustion.

When I appeared, after the evening service, in front of the Master to offer him evening greetings with Cheongun, he said,

"You are suffering because of the Golden Buddha, aren't you?"

I bowed my head but did not say anything.

"Did you read the written record on the Golden Buddha that is in Geumbul-gak?" asked the Master again.

I answered him that I had not read it. He told me to find a chance to read it, then.

The next morning, when I went to offer him morning greetings along with Cheong-un, he said that he had given word to the people at the Geumbul-gak to allow me to look at the record if I should come there.

I folded my hands and bowed. After leaving his presence, I went straight to the Geumbul-gak. The old monk at the shrine opened a stone chest from which he took out a volume about five inches wide and ten inches long. As he handed me the booklet, I noticed that there was a strong smell of incense on it. (It must have been a preventive against mites and bugs.) On the thick front cover of the volume was written in gold: *The Record of Monk Manjeok's Attaining Buddhahood Through Sosin Gongyang*. The four corners of the jacket were also decorated in gold.

When I opened the book on the first page, I found that the paper that was used was grey in color. It had probably been dyed this color. The writing itself was done in golden paint. I read:

萬寂法名俗名曰耆姓曹氏也金陵出生父未詳母張氏改嫁謝公
仇之家仇有一子名曰信年似與耆各十有餘歲一日母　食于二
兒秘置以毒信之食耆偶窺之而按是貪謝家之財爲我故謀害前
室之子以如此耆不堪悲懷乃自欲將取信之食母見之驚而失色
奪之曰是非汝之食也何取信之食耶信與耆默而不答數日後信
去自家行蹟渺然耆曰信己去家我必携信然後歸家卽以隱身而

為僧改稱萬寂以此為法名住於金陵法林院後移淨願寺無風庵
修法于海賢禪師寂二十四歲之春日我生非大覺之材不如供養
吾身以報佛恩乃燒身而供養佛前時忍降雨沛然不犯寂之燒身
寂光漸漱明忍懸圓光以如月輪會眾見之而　感佛恩癒身病眾曰
是焚之法力所致競擲私財賽錢多積以賽鍍金寂之燒身拜之為
佛然後奉置于金佛閣時唐中宗十六年聖曆二年三月朔日

*Manjeok is his sacred name. His worldly name is Gi
and his family name is Jo. He was born in Geum-reung
but nothing is known about his father. His mother, Jang
by name, was remarried to a man named Sa-gu and gave
birth to a son whom they named Sin. In age he was close
to Gi. They were a little over ten years old each when an
incident happened in the house where they all lived
together. One day, their mother put poison in Sin's rice
bowl when serving the tray to the two boys. Gi happened
to see this and judged that his mother was doing this to
take away the property of the Sa house so that her other
son, Gi, that is, could take advantage of it. This thought
plunged Gi into sadness, whereupon he picked up Sin's
rice bowl and started to eat from it. His mother saw this,
however, and snatching the bowl from him in fright,
scolded him saying it was wrong that he should eat what
belonged to his brother. Neither of the boys said
anything. A few days after, Sin disappeared from the
house. Gi said he would go after Sin and bring him*

home. But he never went back. He became a monk and was given the sacred name Manjeok. He served at a temple in Nanking called Beop-rim won, but later moved to the little temple Mupung-am that belonged to Cheongwon-sa and studied Buddhism under Haegak Daesa. At the age of twenty-four, Manjeok proclaimed that since he did not have the endowments for a great awakening, he would offer himself in sosin gongyang and thus serve Buddha's way. As he was burning himself, there poured down a heavy rain from the sky but the rain could not wet Manjeok's body or extinguish the fire that was burning him. Instead the flame grew bigger, and then suddenly people saw a halo the shape and hue of a full moon form around his head. The people who were gathered there felt the blessing of the Buddha deeply, and all who had any illness were cured. They said that it was the spiritual power emanating from Manjeok's body and offered up large sums of money. The monks covered the burnt body of Manjeok with gold with the money the believers offered up in great amounts and called it "Buddha." This Buddha was later installed in the Geumbul-gak. It was the first day of March in the sixteenth year of the reign of Jungjong, Dang Dynasty.

When I returned to Cheongjeongsil after reading this record, the Master summoned me.

"Did you feel more comfortable after reading the record?" He asked.

"I felt less scared. But I still found sadness and pain on his face," I answered.

The Master nodded his head once or twice and said:

"It is only natural. The record is too brief and incomplete...."

He seemed to know more than was recorded.

"But it is something that happened over twelve hundred years ago. How could anything be known except what is in the record?" I asked him.

Wonhye Daesa said that there were stories that have been handed down among the monks. He said, however, that it was a general rule among them not to discuss these things without a good reason. Maybe it was out of deference and fear for the miracle-working power of the Buddha, he said.

What Master Wonhye subsequently told me is roughly as follows. This was of course a concoction of many stories edited into one tolerably coherent and condensed story by the Master himself.

The story up to the time when Manjeok became a monk is about the same as in the record. But there seemed to be several versions of the motive that made him decide to offer himself to the Buddha's way by self-burning. The story I heard from Wonhye Daesa runs as follows:

When Manjeok first became a monk at Beop-rim won in Nanking, there was an older monk named Chwiroe who took care of Manjeok. He was the Master of *gongyang(offerings)* at the temple. Manjeok was his head disciple in learning Buddhist doctrines.

When Manjeok became eighteen, that is five years after he came to Beop-rim won, Chwiroe died. In order to repay his kindness, Manjeok decided to give up his body to the altar of the Buddha.

When Manjeok told Unbong, the Zen priest at Beop-rim won, however, Unbong discouraged Manjeok in his determination to carry out *sosin* because he could see that Manjeok had a capacity for bigger service to Buddhism.

It was by recommendation of Unbong that Manjeok sought Haegak Daesa, another Zen priest, at Mupung-am of Jeongwon-sa. For five years, he studied and trained under Haegak in a most rigorous and severely self-disciplined way. How great his sacred power had grown, however, cannot be measured in any clear terms.

When Manjeok was twenty-three years old, he had an occasion to go near Nanking, and, while there, ran into Sa-Sin, the brother of his former days, who had left the house fleeing from their mother's murderous intent. Manjeok himself had left the house in search of Sa-Sin, but instead of finding him, had become a monk. Now he was seeing him after ten years. But what a re-encounter it was! Although Manjeok was now delivered of worldly thoughts and sentiments, he could not help feeling a heart-wringing sorrow at seeing his half brother after so many years. It was because Sa-Sin who had been good and gentle as a child had become a leper, the worst punishment one could receive from heaven!

Manjeok took off the beads from his own neck and hung it round Sa-Sin's and returned to his temple right away.

From then on, Manjeok stopped eating any cooked food and, until the next spring, all he ate a day was a dish of sesame seeds, not to mention his performing ablution most faithfully during this period.

On the first day of February the next year, he performed the Chwidan-sik ceremony of mounting the altar attended only by the Zen priest Unbong and another elder monk, the Master of Offerings. First, he took off his clothes. His naked body was then bound up, from the tips of his toes to his shoulders, with thin strips of clean white silk. Only his head from the neck upwards was left unbound. He mounted the altar then and sat in the *gabu-jwa* position folding his hands in the front. At the same time as he started chanting a prayer, the Master of Offerings started pouring oil from a jug he was holding in his hands.

When all the oil was poured and the ceremony ended, the two elder monks folded their hands in *hapjang* and left the place.

Oil-soaked, Manjeok stayed like that for one full month. He was turning into a live fossil in his *gabujwa* position with this hands folded in *hapjang*.

Once in seven days, the Master of Offerings came with his jug of wild sesame oil and entered through the curtains which had been hung to keep Manjeok in seclusion. The Master of Offerings poured the oil down from Manjeok's shoulders and went back after all the oil was poured.

After one full month was spent like this, it was time for the sacred service to take place. In order to take part in this special service, a great number of believers, not to mention all the monks on the mountain, gathered from around the area. The spacious courtyard in front of the main hall of Jeongwon-sa filled up with all this crowd that day.

The Sosin Gangyang started at the beginning of the Seventh Hour (from 11a.m. to 1p.m.) when the white curtains were drawn away. Five hundred monks stood facing the altar folding their hands in *hapjang*. The Master of Offerings came out with an incense-burner with burning coals in it and, approaching the altar, lowered it on Manjeok's head. At the same time, all the monks who were standing with folded hands started chanting.

From the incense-burner that had been put on Manjeok's head as if it were a wreath of flowers, smoke rose thicker and more profusely as the minutes passed. When the heat of the burning coals penetrated his vertex, his body twitched involuntarily in spite of the fact that the long period of purification had turned him nearly into fossil by this time. From this point on, his head and the upper half of his body bent forward little by little almost imperceptibly.

Manjeok's body soaked in the oil of wild sesame seeds took a long time to be consumed by smoke. The five hundred monks, however, never ceased their chanting.

At the end of the Ninth Hour, there was a sudden downpour of rain. But strangely, the rain did not fall on the altar on which Manjeok sat, and in fact, more smoke rose from his head into the sky at this time.

The monks and the believers were all astounded by this and did not know what to think. When they turned their eyes back to Manjeok, however, they saw that there was a moonlike halo at the back of his head.

Money poured in from that day on and did not cease for three whole years.

Using this money, the monks plated Manjeok's body, which had settled into a complete fossil in its half burnt state, with gold. With part of the money, they also had the Geumbul-gak and the stone terrace built....

While I listened to this story, related by the Master, I told myself that if this was how the golden Buddha came into being, it was natural for it to look just like the way it looked. I also thought that it was perhaps well that out of a multitude of Buddhas, there was one who was capable of showing so much sorrow and suffering so vividly!

Wonhye Daesa seemed finished with the story-telling now. He said to me out of blue:

"Would you show me the index finger of your right hand?"

This was so sudden and so unrelated to anything we had been talking about—Geumbul-gak, Deungsin-bul, Manjeok's *sosin gongyang*, etc.—that I was more than a little bewildered at first. I showed him, however, the finger which I had bitten to write the characters in blood to present to Mr. Jin Gi-su more than a month ago.

He gazed at it for a long while but he did not say anything. He did not tell me why he asked me to show him the finger, what relation it had with the story of Manjeok, or even whether I was now allowed to put my finger down. We remained in silence.

The big drum was announcing midday from the

Taeheoru interlocked with the sound of the *mok-eo*[7] in a discontented growl.

---

7 Wooden chime in the shape of a fish commonly seen in Buddhist temples.

About the author

Kim Dong-ni (1913-1995), born in Gyeongju,
Gyeongsangbuk-do province, began his literary career at the
age of 16 by publishing several poems in various leading
newspapers. It was through his short stories, however,
that he decisively distinguished himself as a young rising
star in the Korean literary world. In proving himself as one of
the most prolific writers of contemporary Korea, Kim
also received numerous literary awards that acknowledge
his unique achievement as a writer who knows, loves and
portrays the essence of traditional and native Korean themes.

About the translator

Sol Soonbong was born and grew up in Seoul, Korea. She studied English literature at Seoul National University and at Miami University in Oxford, Ohio. Her translations of Korean literature into English include numerous short stories and four novels, one of which is by Kim Dong-ni.